SANTA ANA PUBLIC LIBRARY

AR PTS: 0.5

D1164834

PUBLICATIONS

Extreme Cuisine
Bug-a-licious

by Meish Goldish

Consultants:
David George Gordon, author of *The Eat-a-Bug Cookbook*
Andrew Zimmern, co-creator and host of *Bizarre Foods with Andrew Zimmern*

BEARPORT
PUBLISHING

New York, New York

Credits

Cover and Title Page, © J. Meul/Arco Images GmbH/Alamy; 4, © M. & C. Photography/ Peter Arnold; 5, © Peter Menzel/from the book "Man Eating Bugs"/www.menzelphoto. com; 6, © A.N.T. Photo Library/NHPA/Photoshot; 7, © Oliver Strewe/Corbis; 8, © J. Meul/Arco Images GmbH/Alamy; 9, Courtesy of Yahoo News; 10, © David Wrobel/ Visuals Unlimited; 11, © Peter Menzel/from the book "Man Eating Bugs"/www. menzelphoto.com; 12, © Dwight Kuhn/Dwight Kuhn Photography; 13, © Peter Menzel/from the book "Man Eating Bugs"/www.menzelphoto.com; 14L, © Doug Lemke/Shutterstock; 14R, © Peter Menzel/from the book "Man Eating Bugs"/www. menzelphoto.com; 15, © Peter Menzel/from the book "Man Eating Bugs"/www. menzelphoto.com; 16L, © Peter Menzel/from the book "Man Eating Bugs"/www. menzelphoto.com; 16R, © Oxford Scientific/Photolibrary; 17, © Mona Lisa Productions/ Photolibrary; 18, © David Kuhn/Dwight Kuhn Photography; 19, © Peter Menzel/from the book "Man Eating Bugs"/www.menzelphoto.com; 20, © Creatas/SuperStock; 21, © Michael Freeman/Corbis; 23TL, © Dusan Zidar/Shutterstock; 23TR, © Thomas M. Perkins/Shutterstock; 23C, © Yaroslav/Shutterstock; 23BR, © Lori Skelton/Shutterstock; 23BL, © A. J. Gallant/Shutterstock; 24, © A.N.T. Photo Library/NHPA/Photoshot.

Publisher: Kenn Goin
Editorial Director: Adam Siegel
Creative Director: Spencer Brinker
Design: Debrah Kaiser
Photo Researcher: Laura Saravia

Library of Congress Cataloging-in-Publication Data

Goldish, Meish.
  Bug-a-licious / by Meish Goldish.
    p. cm. — (Extreme cuisine)
  Includes bibliographical references and index.
  ISBN-13: 978-1-59716-757-4 (lib. binding)
  ISBN-10: 1-59716-757-6 (lib. binding)
  1. Cookery (Insects)—Juvenile literature. 2. Edible insects—Juvenile literature.
  3. Cookery, International—Juvenile literature. I. Title.

TX746.G65 2009
641.6'96—dc22

2008032802

Copyright © 2009 Bearport Publishing Company, Inc. All rights reserved. No part of this publication may be reproduced in whole or in part, stored in a retrieval system, or transmitted in any form or by any means, electronic, mechanical, photocopying, recording, or otherwise, without written permission from the publisher.

For more information, write to Bearport Publishing Company, Inc., 101 Fifth Avenue, Suite 6R, New York, New York 10003. Printed in the United States of America.

10 9 8 7 6 5 4 3 2 1

~ MENU ~

Bug Pizza

People love to eat pizza. Many top it with mushrooms or pepperoni. In Mexico, some people put leaf-footed bugs on top. That's right! In lots of countries, **insects** are a popular food. They're crunchy, tasty—and healthy, too. Many insects are a good source of protein, vitamins, and minerals. They are also often low in fat.

Of course, not everyone eats insects. The idea makes some people sick. Yet the world is a big place. One eater's "yuck!" is another eater's "yum!"

leaf-footed bug

More than 1,700 kinds of insects are eaten in over 100 countries around the world.

Honey Ants

Many people buy cookies or ice cream when they want a sweet snack. Others just go digging for honey ants. Aborigines (ab-uh-RIJ-uh-neez), the first people to live in Australia, have been hunting and eating them for thousands of years.

Honey ants taste good because they drink a sweet liquid from plants called **nectar**. They bring it back to their underground nest and feed it to other ants. The nectar is stored in a sac at the rear of their bodies.

Aborigines dig into the ground with sticks and shovels to find these plump ants. They then eat the insects by holding their heads and biting off the nectar bags. Mmmm! The sweet sacs make a sweet snack!

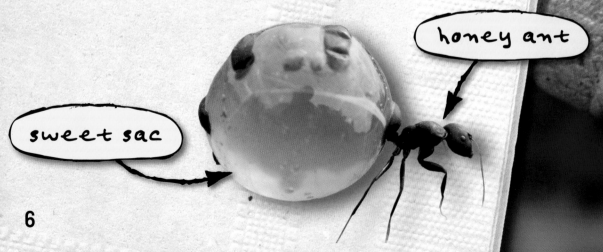

honey ant

sweet sac

In Colombia, South America, movie theaters sell roasted ants instead of popcorn.

Wasp Crackers

People often eat crackers with peanut butter or cheese. In Japan, they eat crackers made with digger wasps!

Hunters catch the insects in forests near the Japanese village of Omachi. The wasps are boiled and dried. Then they are baked in a rice cracker **dough**. Each cracker has at least five or six wasps in it. Young people aren't so eager to eat them. Older people, however, love the tasty snack.

digger wasp

In Japan,
canned wasps are
sold in stores.

9

Water Bug Snacks

Giant water bugs look scary. Yet shoppers in Thailand aren't afraid of them. They go to the market to buy them for food. The insects are boiled and salted. Many people eat them as a snack.

Other people in Thailand dip the giant bugs in batter, fry them, and serve them with a sweet plum sauce. The bugs aren't just tasty. They are also a good way to get iron—which helps carry oxygen from the lungs to other parts of a person's body. In fact, water bugs have four times as much iron as beef!

giant water bug

Giant water bugs in Thailand are about three inches (7.6 cm) long. They're one of the largest bugs in Southeast Asia.

Grasshopper Tacos

In Mexico, some tacos have beef and cheese inside. Others have grasshoppers! The insects are sold all over the country. Shoppers buy them by the bag at markets. They eat the bugs dried or fried.

A grasshopper taco is easy to make. First, the insects are roasted for ten minutes. The green bugs turn red after being cooked. Then they are tossed with lemon juice, garlic, and salt. Finally, the grasshoppers are placed in a corn tortilla with mashed **avocados**. It's a tasty, healthy meal!

grasshopper

Grasshoppers are the most commonly eaten insect in the world.

Dragonflies on a Stick

People who like fast food should love dragonflies. They are really fast food! This speedy insect can fly so quickly—up to 35 miles per hour (56 kph)—that it's hard to catch.

On the island of Bali, people use a stick to trap dragonflies. They cover the stick with gooey **sap** from a tree. When a dragonfly comes near, the hunter touches the insect with the stick. Now it's stuck—and ready to be cooked.

There are many ways to prepare dragonflies. Some people grill them. Others boil the bugs in coconut milk, ginger, and garlic. Still others fry them in coconut oil and eat them like candy!

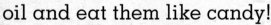

dragonfly

dragonflies caught on a stick

14

fried dragonflies

A dragonfly's
wings are removed
before the insect
is boiled or fried.

Tasty Termites

Termites eat wood, so they can destroy a wooden house. In many African countries, however, some people don't let that happen. They eat the termites first!

In Uganda, people catch termites by poking holes in a termite mound. Next, they place cloths over the holes and grab the termites when they come out. Then they eat the bugs raw.

Some people cook termites before eating them. In Nigeria, people roast the wood-eating insects. In Ghana, the bugs are fried, roasted, or baked in bread.

termite hunting

termites

Some people say that termites taste like sweetened cream. Others describe the crunchy insects as having a nutty flavor.

Spreadable Stink Bugs

Many people don't like food that stinks. Yet stink bugs make a great meal. In South Africa, people collect the bugs early in the morning. To make the bugs get rid of their horrible smell, they put them in a bucket of warm water. The stink-free bugs are then boiled and later dried in the sun. Many South Africans love to snack on the dried insects.

Some people in Mexico like to cook with stink bugs, too. In one dish, roasted stink bugs are mixed with chopped-up chicken livers to make a creamy spread called paté. There's nothing stinky about that!

stink bug

The smell from stink bugs is so strong that people must turn their heads and close their eyes while the insects release their smell in the warm water.

Lick a Cricket

Most people in the United States don't eat insects. One candy maker in California, however, hopes to change their minds. The HotLix candy company makes lollipops with crickets inside. The Cricket Lick-Its come in many flavors, including grape, mint, and orange. HotLix also sells ants swirled in chocolate. The company has grown over the years. Who knows? In the future, more Americans might just "catch the bug" to eat insects!

cricket

Not all insects are safe to eat. Some carry poisons or parasites—small living things found in animals—that can be dangerous to people.

Where Are They Eaten?

Here are some of the places where
bug-a-licious treats are eaten.

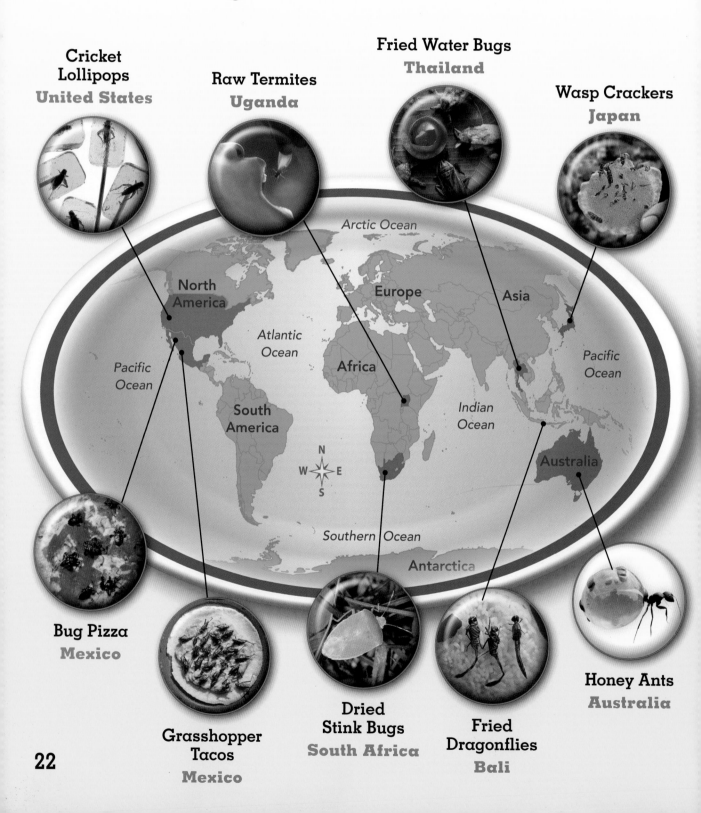

Cricket
Lollipops
United States

Raw Termites
Uganda

Fried Water Bugs
Thailand

Wasp Crackers
Japan

Arctic Ocean

North
America

Europe

Asia

Atlantic
Ocean

Africa

Pacific
Ocean

Pacific
Ocean

South
America

Indian
Ocean

N
W · E
S

Australia

Southern Ocean

Antarctica

Bug Pizza
Mexico

Grasshopper
Tacos
Mexico

Dried
Stink Bugs
South Africa

Fried
Dragonflies
Bali

Honey Ants
Australia

Glossary

avocados (ah-vuh-KAH-dohz)
fruit shaped like a pear with a
tough green or black skin and
a soft green inside

dough (DOH)
a sticky, thick mixture
of flour and water
used to make cookies,
crackers, and bread

insects (IN-sekts)
small animals that have six
legs, three main body parts,
two antennas, and a hard
covering called an exoskeleton

nectar (NEK-tur)
a sweet liquid
found in flowers

sap (SAP)
a liquid that flows through
a plant and carries water
and food for the plant

Index

Bibliography

Gordon, David George. *The Eat-a-Bug Cookbook: 33 Ways to Cook Grasshoppers, Ants, Water Bugs, Spiders, Centipedes, and Their Kin.* Berkeley, CA: Ten Speed Press (1998).

Menzel, Peter, and Faith D'Aluisio. *Man Eating Bugs: The Art and Science of Eating Insects.* Berkeley, CA: Ten Speed Press (1998).

Ramos-Elorduy, Julieta. *Creepy Crawly Cuisine: The Gourmet Guide to Edible Insects.* Rochester, VT: Park Street Press (1998).

Read More

Miller, Connie Colwell. *Disgusting Foods.* Mankato, MN: Capstone Press (2007).

Solheim, James. *It's Disgusting and We Ate It!: True Food Facts from Around the World and Throughout History.* New York: Simon & Schuster (2001).

Learn More Online

To learn more about bug-a-licious treats, visit
www.bearportpublishing.com/ExtremeCuisine

About the Author

Meish Goldish has written more than 100 books for children. He lives in Brooklyn, New York.